Let's Make a

Volcano

by Katie Chanez

NORWOOD HOUSE PRESS

Norwood House Press

For information regarding Norwood House Press, please visit our website at:
www.norwoodhousepress.com or call 866-565-2900.

PHOTO CREDITS: Cover: © Red Line Editorial; © fboudrias/Shutterstock Images, 4; © fmajor/iStockphoto, 12; © gadaian/
iStockphoto, 16; © Justinreznick/iStockphoto, 11; © mikeuk/iStockphoto, 19; © Naeblys/iStockphoto, 7; © Nicolas Primola/
Shutterstock Images, 15; © Red Line Editorial, 21, 23, 24, 25, 26, 27, 28; © Tammy616/iStockphoto, 8

Hardcover ISBN: 978-1-68450-838-9
Paperback ISBN: 978-1-68404-624-9

LIBRARY OF CONGRESS CATALOGING-IN-PUBLICATION DATA

Names: Chanez, Katie, author.
Title: Let's make a volcano / by Katie Chanez.
Description: Chicago : Norwood House Press, 2021. | Series: Make your own: science experiment! | Includes bibliographical
    references and index. | Audience: Grades 2-3.
Identifiers: LCCN 2019053625 (print) | LCCN 2019053626 (ebook) | ISBN 9781684508389 (hardcover) | ISBN 9781684046249
    (paperback) | ISBN 9781684046300 (ebook)
Subjects: LCSH: Volcanoes--Juvenile literature. | Science projects--Juvenile literature. | Science--Experiments--Juvenile literature.
Classification: LCC QE521.3 .C465 2021 (print) | LCC QE521.3 (ebook) | DDC 551.21--dc23
LC record available at https://lccn.loc.gov/2019053625
LC ebook record available at https://lccn.loc.gov/2019053626

328N—072020
Manufactured in the United States of America in North Mankato, Minnesota.

Contents

It is dangerous to get too close to an erupting volcano.

CHAPTER 1

All about Volcanoes

A mountain has been smoking for several days. Suddenly there is a loud explosion. Fire, melted rock, and ash shoot into the sky. The melted rock begins to run down the sides of the mountain. A volcano has **erupted**!

A volcano is an opening in Earth's **crust**. Sometimes these openings are covered by mountains. Beneath the crust is a layer of extremely hot rock. This layer is called the mantle. Most of the rock in the mantle stays solid. But some melts. This liquid rock is called **magma**. Volcanoes allow gas and melted rock to reach Earth's surface.

Earth's crust is made of huge sections called **tectonic plates**. The plates move across the mantle. When plates move apart, magma rises to fill the empty space. It cools to create new crust. When the plates collide, sometimes one is pushed under the other. The plate underneath melts into magma. Volcanoes usually form near plate edges.

Sometimes the mantle has hot spots. These are places where unusually hot magma rises from deep underground. Hot spots can

All of Earth's surface is divided into tectonic plates.

melt the crust in places where normal magma does not. Hawaii
is a chain of islands that are actually volcanoes. It was formed
over a hot spot. The crust over the hot spot melted. This created
a volcano. The plate continued to move. New volcanoes formed.

The oldest volcanoes are no longer over the hot spot. They have stopped erupting.

Other volcanoes form when magma pools in Earth's crust. Magma rises above the solid rock in the mantle. Magma rises because it is less **dense** than the solid rock around it. As it rises, it melts more rock. The magma gathers in the crust just under the surface. It pools in **magma chambers**. These are large openings under the volcano. More and more magma flows into the chamber. Magma has gases trapped inside. As the magma rises, less weight pushes down on the gases. The gases form bubbles. This builds **pressure**. When there is enough pressure, the volcano erupts.

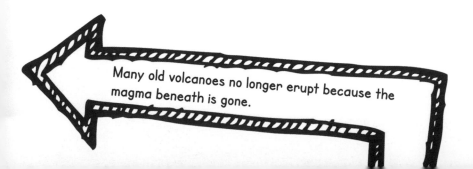
Many old volcanoes no longer erupt because the magma beneath is gone.

The volcano you build will work in a similar way. Gas will build up. This will make your homemade magma rise and spill out of a bottle.

Magma that reaches Earth's surface is called **lava**. Volcanoes release a super-hot mix of lava, solid rocks, ash, and gas during an eruption. This mix cools around the opening. It hardens to form the shape of the volcano.

There are three basic kinds of volcanoes. Cinder cones are small volcanoes. Lava is thrown high in the air and falls around the opening. This creates a circle- or oval-shaped cone with straight sides. Shield volcanoes form when the lava is thin. When a shield volcano erupts, the lava flows in all directions instead of exploding. This creates a flat dome. The dome's sides gently slope down, like a shield.

Lava cools to form several types of rocks, depending on the conditions.

Most volcanoes are stratovolcanoes. These volcanoes usually have thick lava. It does not flow easily. The magma cannot easily reach the surface, and it plugs up the opening of the volcano. A lot of pressure is needed to force the magma out. This causes

Stratovolcanoes form tall and steep mountains.

explosive eruptions. The lava collects around the opening in the crust.
A tall, steep volcano forms. Sometimes volcanoes collapse. This forms
large craters called calderas.

One of the most famous eruptions was Mount Vesuvius in 79 CE. The nearby city of Pompeii was destroyed. Another famous eruption was Krakatoa. Krakatoa was a volcano on an island off the coast of Indonesia. It erupted in 1883. The explosion is the loudest sound ever recorded. It could be heard in Australia, over 1,900 miles (3,000 km) away. Nearly 70 percent of the island was destroyed. Gases released in the explosion changed weather patterns all over the world for several years.

Volcanic eruptions are measured on a scale called Volcanic Explosivity Index (VEI). This scale runs from VEI 1 to VEI 8. VEI 8 is the most powerful. Scientists believe there have only been 42 eruptions that powerful. The last VEI 8 eruption was 70,000 years ago.

Volcanoes that erupt this strongly are called supervolcanoes. Yellowstone National Park in Wyoming is a supervolcano. Its last eruption was 640,000 years ago. The volcano collapsed and formed a caldera.

Most volcanoes do not erupt very often. Some may never erupt again. Scientists have divided volcanoes into three categories. Active volcanoes have erupted in the past 10,000 years. The Kilauea volcano in Hawaii is active. It erupted continually from 1983 to 2018. Dormant volcanoes have not erupted during the last 10,000 years, but scientists believe they will one day. Mount Kilimanjaro in Tanzania is a dormant volcano. It was active 200,000 years ago. Extinct volcanoes are not expected to erupt again. Mount Kenya in Kenya is an extinct volcano.

How a Volcano Erupts

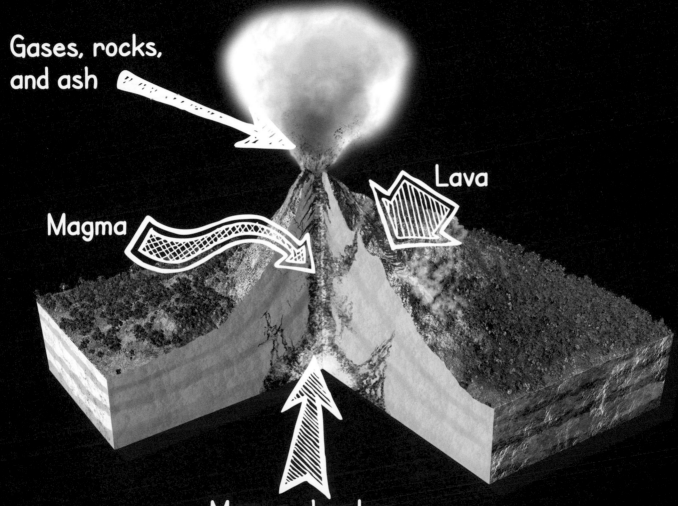

Gases, rocks, and ash

Lava

Magma

Magma chamber

Strong pressure pushes gases, rocks, and ash high into the sky.

CHAPTER 2

Make Your Own Volcano

Volcanic eruptions are dangerous, with superheated lava, rocks, gas, and ash. You need ingredients that are safe but that will still create an eruption. Your volcano will use a **chemical reaction** to build pressure.

Magma gathers in chambers before an eruption. You need a place to combine your ingredients, like a magma chamber.

You need a material that will not absorb the liquid. A plastic bottle is designed to hold liquids. It will be your magma chamber.

Magma chambers are deep in the ground or inside mountains. You need something to cover your chamber to make a mountain. The cover needs to easily make a cone shape. Paper is easy to shape, but it will absorb liquid. Modeling clay is also easy to shape. The clay will let the lava flow down the sides.

Volcanoes erupt when the magma and gas build pressure. The pressure builds until the magma bursts to Earth's surface. You will also use gas to build pressure. This will cause your volcano's eruption. You will mix an **acid** and a **base** to create the gas.

Trapped gases form tiny holes in volcanic rock when lava cools.

Mixing an acid with a base causes a chemical reaction. New materials are formed. Vinegar is an acid. You will combine it with baking soda. Baking soda is a base. The gas **carbon dioxide** forms when the two are mixed. Carbon dioxide is one of the many gases that volcanoes release when they erupt.

Gas is trapped in magma and then released during a real eruption. You need something to trap the gas. Dish soap is safe. It holds bubbles of gas. This will make the lava foamy. The gas and soap mixture will begin to rise. It will come out the top of your volcano when there is too much pressure.

If possible, make your volcano outside. It will be easier to clean up. Or you can put your volcano in a large pan to catch the lava. Have an adult help you. Once your ingredients are combined, step back and watch your eruption go!

Materials Checklist

- ✓ Modeling clay
- ✓ Plastic bottle
- ✓ Vinegar
- ✓ Red food coloring
- ✓ Liquid dish soap
- ✓ Water
- ✓ Baking soda
- ✓ Spoon
- ✓ Funnel
- ✓ 1/2 cup measuring cup
- ✓ Large pan (optional)

Try flattening your clay first. Then wrap it around the bottle.

CHAPTER **3**

Science Experiment!

Now that you know what makes volcanoes erupt, put your knowledge to use and make your own!

1. Take the lid off the plastic bottle. Use the modeling clay to form a cone around the bottle. Do not cover the bottle's opening.

2. Fill the bottle halfway with about 1 cup of warm water.

3. Add a spoonful of the liquid dish soap.

4. Add red food coloring. This will make it look like lava.

5. Slowly pour about 1/2 cup of vinegar into the bottle until the bottle is 3/4 full.

6. Carefully add two spoonfuls of baking soda.

7. Quickly step back and watch your eruption!

8. When the eruption slows down, you can add more vinegar and baking soda to keep it going.

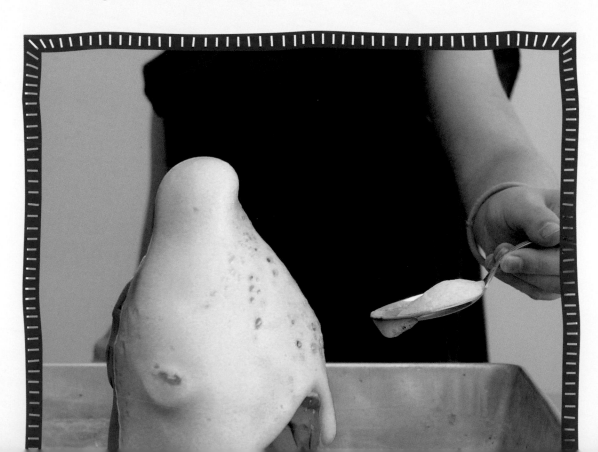

Make It Better!

Congratulations! You have made a volcano erupt. Now see if there are ways to improve it. Use any of these changes and see how they improve your volcano.

- This version of a volcano used vinegar as the acid. Many other acids create carbon dioxide when mixed with baking soda. Lemon juice or ketchup are two examples. How does changing the acid affect the speed of your eruption?

- Try to make a bigger eruption. How will you have to adjust the amounts of the ingredients?

Can you think of any ways that you could improve or change your volcano to make it better?

Glossary

acid (A-sid): A chemical that breaks down metals and tastes sour.

base (BAYSS): A substance that forms a chemical reaction with acids.

carbon dioxide (KAR-buhn dy-OK-syd): A colorless gas made of carbon and oxygen.

chemical reaction (KEM-uh-kuhl ree-AK-shuhn): A process in which the atoms in ingredients rearrange into something else.

crust (KRUST): The outermost layer of Earth.

dense (DENSS): Thick or heavy for its size.

erupted (i-RUHPT-ed): To have released something suddenly.

lava (LAH-vuh): Magma after it reaches Earth's surface.

magma (MAG-muh): Melted rock beneath Earth's surface.

magma chambers (MAG-muh CHAYM-burz): Places under Earth's surface where magma gathers.

pressure (PRESH-ur): The force of something pressing against something else.

tectonic plates (tek-TAWN-ik PLAYTSS): Large pieces of Earth's crust that move over the mantle.

For More Information

Books

Alicia Klepeis. *The Science of Volcanic Eruptions*. New York, NY: Cavendish Square, 2020. This book explains how volcanic eruptions happen and the effects eruptions have on people and the environment.

Joan Galat. *Erupt! 100 Fun Facts about Volcanoes*. Washington, DC: National Geographic Children's Books, 2017. This book explores how volcanoes form and erupt, with fun facts throughout.

Karina Hamalainen. *Hawai'i Volcanoes*. New York, NY: Children's Press, 2019. Readers learn about Hawai'i Volcanoes National Park.

Websites

DK Find Out: How a Volcano Erupts (https://www.dkfindout.com/us/earth/volcanoes/how-volcano-erupts/) This interactive infographic explains how a volcano erupts.

NASA Space Place: What Is a Volcano? (https://spaceplace.nasa.gov/volcanoes2/en/) This article teaches students about different types of volcanoes.

National Geographic Kids: 17 Explosive Volcano Facts! (https://www.natgeokids.com/uk/discover/geography/physical-geography/volcano-facts/) Students will learn fun facts about volcanoes.

Index

About the Author

Katie Chanez is a children's book writer and editor originally from Iowa. She enjoys writing fiction, playing with her cat, and petting friendly dogs. Katie now lives and works in Minnesota.